27

 **W9-BMY-111**

FORCES
and MOTION

Rebecca Hunter

First published in 2003 by Franklin Watts
Franklin Watts, 96 Leonard Street, London EC2A 4XD

Franklin Watts Australia
45–51 Huntley Street, Alexandria, NSW 2015
This edition published under license from Franklin Watts.
All rights reserved.

Editor: Rebecca Hunter; Design: Keith Williams; Consultant:
Jeremy Bloomfield; Illustrations: Stefan Chabluk: page 16;
Keith Williams: pages 21–22, 26–27

Published in the United States by Smart Apple Media
1980 Lookout Drive, North Mankato, Minnesota 56003

Library of Congress Cataloging-in-Publication Data

Hunter, Rebecca (Rebecca K. de C.)
The facts about forces and motion / Rebecca Hunter.
p. cm. — (Science the facts)
Includes index.
Contents: What is a force?—Friction—Air and water resistance—Gravity—Gravity outside the earth—Upthrust—Forces
in motion—Measuring forces—Magnetism—Magnetic
earth—Living with forces—Making forces work for us—
Forces around us.
ISBN 1-58340-451-1
1. Force and energy—Juvenile literature. 2. Motion—Juvenile
literature. [1. Force and energy. 2. Motion.] I Title: Forces
and Motion. II. Title. III. Series.

QC73.4.H87 2004
531'.6—dc22   2003059157

9 8 7 6 5 4 3 2 1

Photographs:
Bruce Coleman: cover, page 5, page 8 (Christer
Fredriksson), page 9 top, page 11, page 12, page 17,
page 22, page 29 (Jeff Foott); Corbis: page 14, page
16; Discovery Picture Library: page 4, page 19 top,
page 20 bottom, page 28 bottom; Impact Photos: page 7
(Ken Graham); Mary Evans Picture Library: page 18;
NASA: page 13, page 28; Oxford Scientific Films: page
10 (Bernd Schellhammer), page 15 (Laurence Gould), page
25 (Alain Christof); Photodisc: page 9 bottom; Rebecca
Hunter: page 6, page 19 bottom; Science Photo Library:
page 20 top (Richard Megna), page 23 (Cordelia Molloy),
page 24 (James Stevenson), page 27 (John Howard), page
28 right.

the facts about
FORCES
and MOTION

Contents

Words in **bold** appear in the glossary on page 30.

What is a force?

A force is a push or a pull. You cannot see forces, but you can see the effect they have on things.

A force makes something move. Once an object starts moving, it will keep moving until another force stops it. There are four ways in which forces act on things: they can make them speed up, slow down, change direction, or change shape.

Speeding up and slowing down

If you are riding a bicycle and want to go faster, you have to pedal harder. You use more force, which makes you speed up. When you want to slow down, you use the brakes. These produce a force of **friction** that slows the wheels. The bicycle will slow down and eventually stop.

Changing direction

When you hit a ball, you use force to change the way it is moving. A tennis player hits a ball that is moving toward him or her. The ball then changes direction and moves away.

A twisting movement is a force that makes something rotate. When you need to open a jar, you twist the lid one way. Twisting it the opposite way closes it.

Changing shape

A force can also change the shape of something. Squeezing or stretching things can alter their shape. Some things squeeze or stretch more easily than others.

► These yachts have many forces working on them, including both **upthrust** from the water and the movement of the wind.

It is easy to stretch elastic or squeeze a sponge. It is not easy to squeeze or stretch wood, iron, or steel. Steel can be stretched only if it is made into a spring. When springs are pulled by a force, they stretch. When the force is removed, the spring returns to its original shape.

There are other forces at work around us, too. Boats float because of the force of water pushing upward. **Compasses** work because of the force of **magnetism**. The force of friction makes things grip. We stay on the surface of Earth because of the force of **gravity**. You will find out about all these forces in this book.

key facts

- ⟳ A force is a push or pull.

- ⟳ Forces make things speed up, slow down, change direction, or change shape.

- ⟳ Friction, magnetism, and gravity are all forces.

Friction

Friction is a force that occurs when two surfaces rub against each other.

When this happens, the two surfaces stick to each other a little—they grip each other. This grip slows the movement down.

If you push a toy car along the floor, it will start off traveling fast but will soon slow down and stop. This is due to the force of friction between the car's wheels and the floor.

The amount of friction depends on the type of surface. Rough surfaces slow things down more quickly, so we say the friction between them is greater. Smooth surfaces slide over each other easily—the amount of friction between them is small.

Useful friction

Friction is a very useful force. Without it you would not be able to pick anything up: things would just slide out of your hands. People would fall over, and cars and airplanes would not be able to stop!

We make use of friction all the time. Outdoor shoes have deep treads on the sole so people can walk safely on slippery, wet pavements or climb muddy hills without falling over. The deeper the tread, the more the shoe grips the ground.

▼ A tractor needs large tires with deep treads to give it a good grip on a plowed field.

Cars have treads on their tires to give them good grip on wet roads. It is dangerous to drive when the tread has worn down.

Sometimes we want to reduce friction as much as possible to allow things to go faster. Skiers polish their skis to make them as smooth as possible so they can move quickly over the snow.

▼ There is very little friction between skis and snow, enabling skiers to move very fast.

Friction and heat

Friction produces heat. You can prove this yourself by rubbing your hands together. They will soon feel warm.

Sometimes the heat produced by friction can be a nuisance, or even dangerous. Most machines have moving parts. They are usually covered in oil and grease to reduce friction. Without this, the parts would soon wear out, and in some cases, the heat produced by friction could start a fire.

key facts

- Friction acts when two surfaces touch each other.
- Friction slows things down.
- Friction gives us grip.
- Friction produces heat.

Air and water resistance

Things that move are slowed down not only by the surface they move on (friction), but also by the substance they pass through. Both air and water create drag, or resistance.

When a leaf falls from a tree, it doesn't plunge straight down as a stone would; it floats gently. This is because air is pushing up against the surface of the leaf. The bigger the **surface area**, the greater the air resistance. A big leaf encounters more air resistance than a small one and therefore takes longer to fall.

▶ Paragliders make use of air resistance to slow their fall.
The open canopy has a very large surface area so it encounters a lot of air resistance.

Streamlining

If something needs to travel fast through the air, it must be streamlined. This means it has a smooth, slim shape that offers the least resistance to the air. Rockets, airplanes, arrows, and bullets all have streamlined shapes and can travel at very high speeds.

Birds also need to move easily through the air. Looking at the shape of fast-moving birds such as swallows or hawks, it's easy to see how they are streamlined. Most flightless birds do not need to be streamlined. An ostrich is obviously not designed to fly!

◄ A jet boat is designed to move as fast as possible over water.

Water resistance

Water creates a greater resistance than air, so to move through water, objects also need to be streamlined. Speedboats are pointed and smooth so they can move fast over the water. Although a rowboat is not built for speed, it still needs a pointed bow to be able to move across the water.

Animals that live in the water often have very similar shapes. The shapes of a dolphin (mammal), a shark (fish), and a penguin (bird) are all very similar. Their shape enables them to move quickly and easily underwater.

key facts

- Air resistance slows things down.

- Water resistance is greater than air resistance.

- Streamlined objects can move faster through the air and through water.

Gravity

Gravity is the force that keeps you on the ground. Without gravity you would fly off into space!

Gravity pulls everything toward the center of Earth. It is the force that makes things fall when they are dropped. When you throw a ball in the air, your throw pushes the ball upward. The force of your throw takes the ball only so high. The pull of gravity slows the ball down and pulls it back to the ground. All things on Earth are affected by gravity. It affects things in the air, in water, and on the ground.

However, things that are the same size do not always weigh the same: big things are not necessarily heavier than small things. A balloon is much lighter than a watermelon of the same size. A television set is smaller, but much heavier, than an inflated air bed. This makes it difficult to judge the weight of something just by looking at it.

Weight

Heavy objects are pulled strongly toward the center of Earth by gravity. A light object is not being pulled as strongly. Gravity pulling down on an object gives it weight.

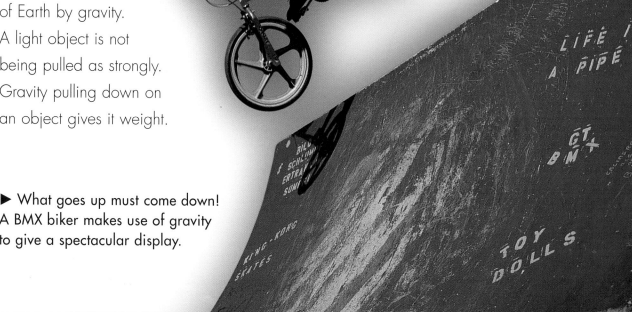

▶ What goes up must come down! A BMX biker makes use of gravity to give a spectacular display.

Discovering gravity

You might think that heavier things fall to Earth faster than lighter things. However, 400 years ago an Italian scientist named Galileo did an experiment to show that if air resistance is ignored, all things fall at the same speed—whatever their weight. So if a large bowling ball and a small golf ball were dropped off a tall building at the same time, they would reach the ground at the same time. The only thing that can interfere with this rule is air resistance, which as we have seen (*page 8*), acts on things with a large surface area and slows them down.

▲ A pole vaulter needs to use her strength and skills of balance to overcome the force of gravity and to get over the bar.

key facts

- Gravity pulls all things toward the center of Earth.
- Gravity gives things weight.
- All things fall at the same speed.

Gravity outside Earth

Gravity is a force that attracts all objects to each other. The bigger the object, the greater its gravitational force.

In the 17th century, the British scientist Isaac Newton realized that the force that makes things fall to Earth was the same force that keeps the moon **orbiting** around Earth and the planets going around the sun.

Scientists have proved that gravity exists between all the immense objects in space—between stars and between the planets, moons, and **asteroids**.

Escaping gravity

The strength of gravitational force is the same all over Earth. It takes a very powerful force and a lot of speed (called escape velocity) in order to transport people and machines beyond the pull of Earth's gravity.

▼ All the planets in our solar system are held in place around the sun by the force of the sun's gravity.

The space shuttle is almost 31 times more powerful than a jumbo jet; it accelerates to 17,500 miles (28,000 km) per hour to get into orbit above Earth's atmosphere.

▲ There is little gravity on the moon, so astronauts felt almost weightless. The space suits that seemed so cumbersome on Earth became much easier to wear on the moon.

Gravity on the moon

Because the moon is much smaller than Earth, its force of gravity is much less. It is actually one-sixth of the gravity of Earth. This means that the weight of everything on the moon is one-sixth of what it would be on Earth. The space suits that the astronauts wore to the moon felt heavy on Earth, yet almost weightless on the moon.

The world's long jump record is 29.25 feet (8.95 m) on Earth. On the moon it could be as much as 175 feet (54 m)! The large planet Jupiter has a much stronger pull of gravity than Earth. There the jump would not be more than 11 feet (3.4 m).

key facts

- The force of gravity exists in space between stars and planets.

- Earth is kept in orbit around the sun by the sun's force of gravity.

- The force of gravity is much weaker on the moon because it is smaller than Earth.

Upthrust

When something pushes down on water, the water pushes up. The force of water pushing back is called upthrust.

Upthrust is also produced in air, but it is much greater in water. You can feel the upthrust when you try to push a beach ball under the water. When an object is put in water it weighs much less than when it is in the air. This is because the upthrust of the water cancels out some of the force of gravity pulling down.

▼ The upthrust of water keeps this raft, and the children, on the surface of the water.

You can do it...

Prove how upthrust works. Take a blob of Silly Putty and drop it in a sink of water. It will sink. Now make the Silly Putty into the shape of a bowl. Put it into the water again. If it still doesn't float you will need to make the surface area even greater; flatten it out a bit more.

Sinking and floating

An object in water has at least two forces acting on it. Gravity is pulling it down and giving it weight, and upthrust is pushing it up. The force of the upthrust depends on how much water has been pushed out of the way by the object. We say this is the amount of water it displaces. A large object displaces a lot of water, so the upthrust is big. If only a small amount of water is displaced, the upthrust will be smaller than the force of gravity.

The combination of upthrust and weight determines whether an object will sink or float in water. When the upthrust is equal to or greater than the weight, an object will float. If the weight is greater than the upthrust, the object will sink.

▲ Anchors are designed to sink and hold a boat in place. They are made of metal and their weight is much greater than the upthrust of water.

key facts

- The force of water pushing up is called upthrust.

- Upthrust is greater in water than in air.

- The size of upthrust in water depends on the amount of water displaced.

- When upthrust is equal to or greater than its weight, the object will float.

Forces in motion

Everywhere you look there are objects in motion.

Birds and airplanes fly overhead, cars move along roads, people runor walk, trees move inthe wind, rivers flow downhill. Forces act on all things to make them move. Once they are moving, they will continue to move until another force makes them alter speed, change direction, or stop.

▲ The sled will keep moving until friction finally makes it stop.

Size and direction

A force has two parts: size and direction. These can be shown in diagrams with arrows. The stronger the force, the greater the movement.

Combining forces

Many objects are acted on by more than one force. Sometimes forces combine to create one bigger force. For example, when two horses are harnessed together to pull a cart, they each create a forward force. These two forces combine together to produce one large forward force.

◀ Here a ball has been passed to a soccer player with a small force. When he kicks the ball he applies a larger force and changes the direction of the ball.

▲ This sail boat is staying upright because the weight of the crew balances the force of the wind in the sails.

Balanced forces

If an object is still, it doesn't mean there are no forces acting on it. Forces are always in action. If nothing happens when a force acts on an object, it means that the force must be balanced by another force pushing in the opposite direction. We say they are in **equilibrium**.

If the two teams in a tug-of-war are equal in number and strength, the rope will not move: the two forces cancel each other out and produce a balance. If someone else joins one of the teams, that team will now be stronger. It will exert a stronger force and probably win the contest.

key facts

- Forces have two parts: size and direction.

- To make something move, one force must be stronger than another.

- If two forces are equal, they are balanced and the object will not move.

A tent is an example of several forces in equilibrium. The guy ropes and tent pegs at one end pull in opposite directions of those at the other end. Gravity is also pulling the tent downward. As long as the poles and ropes remain in place, the tent will stay up.

Measuring forces

Force is measured in units called **newtons**. The newton is named after Sir Isaac Newton, who was one of the first people who really understood the force of gravity.

We use an instrument called a forcemeter to measure how strong a force is. A forcemeter has a spring inside it. As the spring is stretched, a marker moves along a scale that indicates the size of the stretching force. The scale shows the force in newtons. Forces of up to 100 newtons can be measured using a forcemeter.

One newton is the force needed to lift a small apple. When you kick a ball, the kick applies a force of about 10 newtons.

◀ Sir Isaac Newton (1642–1727) was one of the world's greatest scientists. He developed his ideas about gravity after watching an apple fall from a tree in his orchard.

▼ The force of a jet engine is 100,000 newtons.

Weight and gravity

A set of weighing scales works in the same way as a forcemeter. It is used to measure the pull of gravity on an object. When something is put on the scales, the measurement is actually the pull of gravity on it. A scale can tell the object's weight in both ounces and grams.

key facts

- The unit of force, the newton, is named after Sir Isaac Newton.

- Force is measured with a forcemeter.

- The force of gravity gives things weight.

Magnetism

Magnetism is another invisible force that is easy to see in action. Magnetism is the ability of a piece of metal to attract something to it or push something away from it.

A magnet is a piece of metal that will attract another metal. Metals that contain iron are attracted to magnets and are said to be magnetic. Nickel is also magnetic.

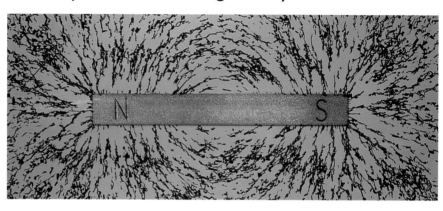

▲ The effect of the magnetic field around a bar magnet can be seen if **iron filings** are sprinkled around the magnet. The iron filings always arrange themselves into the same kind of pattern.

Magnetic poles

All magnets have two ends, or poles. These are called north and south poles. They are sometimes marked on a magnet with the letters N and S. Some magnets are painted so that the north pole is red and the south pole is blue. The north pole of a magnet is always attracted to the south pole of another. Two north or two south poles will push away from, or repel, each other. The area around a magnet (where its magnetic force can be detected) is called a magnetic field.

▲ Magnets come in many shapes and sizes. Refrigerator magnets are most commonly seen around the house.

▲ Bar magnet

▲ Round magnet

▲ Horseshoe magnet

Making magnets

Some magnets keep their magnetism all the time. They are called permanent magnets. Other metals can be made into magnets for a short time. This is because a magnetic metal can be thought of as containing millions of tiny magnets. In a magnet, these are all facing the same way so their magnetism combines as one large magnet. In a non-magnetized metal, they face in different directions so that their magnetism cancels out. It is possible to line the tiny magnets up in a piece of iron or steel and make a magnet.

▼ Magnetized metal

▼ Non-magnetized metal

You can do it...

Make a magnet. Stroke a steel nail with a magnet. Always stroke it with the same end of the magnet, and always stroke in the same direction down the nail. Stroke the nail about 30 times. Now hold the nail over some paper clips. How many will it pick up? If you stroke the nail some more you will make it more magnetic, and it will pick up more paper clips.

key facts

- Magnetism is a force between two magnetic materials.

- Magnets are attracted to certain metals.

- Anything that contains iron will be attracted to a magnet.

Magnetic Earth

Because the center of Earth is made of iron, the planet Earth acts like a giant magnet.

Like a magnet, Earth has two magnetic poles. One of these is close to the North Pole. This is called the magnetic north pole. The magnetic south pole is near the South Pole.

The fact that Earth acts like a giant magnet and has its own magnetic field can be very useful for travelers. This is because any magnet that is allowed to move freely will line itself up so that it points in a north-south direction.

▲ There are many different sorts of compass for use on land, at sea, and underwater.

▲ Earth's magnetic field is similar in shape to that produced by a magnet and iron filings (*see page 20*).

Magnetic compass

A compass consists of a magnetic needle that is balanced so that it swings freely. The needle's south pole points toward Earth's magnetic north pole. This enables travelers to know which direction is north, and therefore which way to go. A compass is especially useful to ships at sea. Since there are no landmarks at sea, sailors rely on a compass to help them **navigate**.

Make your own compass. Make a needle act like a magnet by stroking it with a magnet (*see page 21*). Then float the needle on a piece of cork or polystyrene in a bowl of water. The needle will swing around and point in a north-south direction.

Lodestone

Magnetite is a type of iron ore that is often magnetic. It used to be called lodestone, which means "guiding stone," and was used by sailors as a compass more than 1,000 years ago.

key facts

- Because of its iron center, Earth acts like a giant magnet.

- A compass always points north-south.

- Lodestone is a natural magnet that was used as an early type of compass.

Living with forces

We have to cope with forces every day of our lives. Because we cannot change them, we have to learn to live with them and use them for our own benefit.

Often we have to find the right balance between forces. When you learn to ride a bicycle, you have to cope with the forces of gravity, friction, and air resistance. The force you apply to the pedals drives you forward. If there were no force of friction, you would not be able to move forward and your wheels would just spin and not grip the ground.

If it was a windy day and the force of air resistance was greater than your forward force, you would be blown backward. Or else the force of gravity would pull you to the ground! Fortunately, your forward force is usually greater than air resistance, friction, and gravity, so you are usually able to move in the direction you want.

Forces in buildings

When architects and engineers design buildings and bridges, they have to take into account the forces that will be acting on the structures. If the **foundations** and walls are not strong enough, the structures will bend or fall down.

◀ In parts of the world where **earthquakes** are common, constructing earthquake-resistant buildings can be quite a challenge. This triangular building in San Francisco has been designed to resist earthquakes.

▲ The Pont du Gard in France was built by the Romans in 19 B.C. as an **aqueduct** to carry water to Nîmes. Thanks to its strong arches, it is still standing 2,000 years later.

The triangle is the strongest shape to build with and is used in the construction of many buildings and bridges. An arch is almost as strong as a triangle. Because it is both strong and decorative, it can be found in many large buildings, tunnels, and bridges.

key facts

- ◯ Engineers have to take forces into account when designing buildings.

- ◯ Triangles are the strongest shapes to build with.

- ◯ Buildings can be designed to withstand the forces caused by earthquakes.

Making forces work for us

There are many ways in which forces can be made to work for us. Simple machines work on the principle of using a small force to make a large one.

Levers

If you want to move an object, such as a large rock that is too heavy to move on your own, it is often possible to do it by using a lever. A lever is a long rod propped up on a small object, called a fulcrum. When you push down on the rod at the end furthest from the fulcrum, a greater force is produced at the other end— thus raising the **load**.

Wheel and axle

In a wheel and axle device, a wheel is used to turn an axle that can be used to raise a load. An example of this is the winch system that pulls a bucket out of a well. The handle (the wheel) turns a shaft (the axle) which is attached to a rope and bucket. The winch will lift the load with a greater force than the effort needed to turn the handle.

▼ A lever

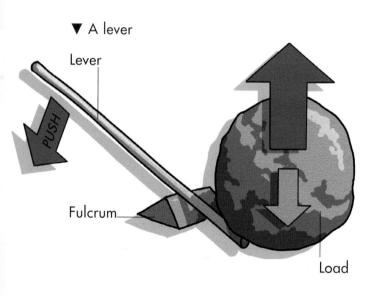

Lever

PUSH

Fulcrum

Load

▼ A wheel and axle

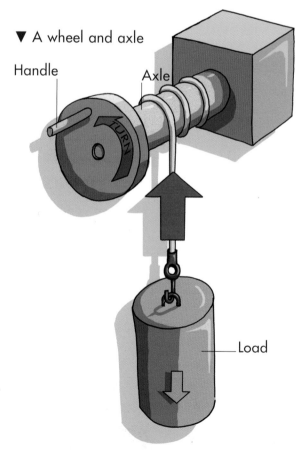

Handle

Axle

TURN

Load

◀ A pulley

Wheels

Load

Pulleys

Another way to lift a heavy load is with a pulley system. This consists of a set of wheels with a rope wound between them. One end of the rope is attached to the load. The other is pulled by a person. The more wheels there are in the pulley system, the easier it is to lift the load.

Gears

Gears are toothed wheels that are locked together in pairs. They can **magnify** speed or force to a greater or lesser extent depending on the size of the wheels and the number of teeth. Gear wheels are at work inside watches and clocks as well as many larger machines.

key facts

- Forces can work for us as well as against us.
- Simple machines use small amounts of force to **generate** large amounts of force.

Forces around us

Forces are needed to start things moving, to change the way they move, and to stop their movement. Without forces and energy, nothing would happen.

The **atmosphere** of a planet or star is kept in place by the force of gravity. Earth's force of gravity holds all of us on the surface of the planet.

A moving object will continue to move until the friction produced by air or water resistance slows it down, and then eventually it will stop.

▼ Magnetism is an invisible force between metal objects. This magnetic sculpture shows how the force of magnetism works on metals containing iron.

▲ A huge amount of energy is needed to launch a rocket into space. This energy is obtained from the rocket's fuel and is converted into an enormous upward force.

There is always more than one force acting on any moving object. What happens to the object depends on which force is strongest. In this picture, the boat is floating because the force of the upthrust of water is greater than the weight of the boat's gravity. The boat is moving forward because the force of movement made by the kayaker is greater than the force of friction the water resistance creates.

key facts

- The world is full of forces.
- Forces make things move.
- Forces can push things apart or hold things together.
- Moving objects have more than one force acting on them.
- The force of gravity holds everything on the planet.
- Friction is a force that causes objects to slow down and stop.
- Magnetism is an invisible force between certain metals.

Glossary

Aqueduct A bridge-like structure built to carry water, usually across a valley.

Asteroid A rocky body that orbits the sun.

Atmosphere A layer of gases that surrounds Earth.

Compass A device that shows the direction of north.

Earthquake A major shaking of Earth.

Equilibrium When two things are in a state of balance.

Foundation The part of a building that is underground.

Friction A force that slows down or stops the movement of one surface against another.

Generate To make or create.

Gravity The force of attraction between two masses. It attracts all things to Earth and gives them weight.

Iron filings Small shavings of iron.

Load An object that needs to be moved or carried.

Magnetism The invisible force of attraction between some substances, especially iron. The substance is said to be magnetic.

Magnify To make bigger.

Navigate To find one's way to a destination.

Newton Force is measured in units called newtons, named after the scientist Sir Isaac Newton.

Orbiting The way in which a planet or satellite goes around another body, such as a star or a planet.

Surface area The area of the outside of something.

Upthrust The upward push on an object in water.

Further information

Books

Gardner, Robert. *Forces and Motion Science Fair Projects Using Water Balloons, Pulleys, and Other Stuff*. Berkeley Heights, New Jersey: Enslow Publishers, 2004.

Richards, Jon. *Forces and Simple Machines*. London: Franklin Watts, 2002.

Richards, Jon. *Magnets*. London: Franklin Watts, 2002.

Tocci, Salvatore. *Experiments With Motion*. New York: Children's Book Press, 2003.

Web sites

Beginner's Guide to Aerodynamics
Learn about the study of forces and the resulting motion of objects through the air. Includes problems to try and an index of topics from NASA.
http://www.lerc.nasa.gov/WWW/K-12/airplane/bga.html

Funderstanding Roller Coaster
How high or fast can you go? Design your own coaster and achieve maximum thrills and chills without crashing or flying off the track by learning about force, friction, and gravity.
http://www.funderstanding.com/k12/ coaster/

Newton's Laws of Motion
Discover more about Newton and his laws of motion.
http://id.mind.net/~zona/mstm/physics/mechanics/forces/newton/newton.html

Physics4Kids
Find out how physics is a part of everything we know! This site has simple explanations of motion, thermodynamics, light, modern physics, and electricity.
http://www.kapili.com/topiclist.html

Places to Visit

U.S.
Adler Planetarium
Chicago, Illinois
http://www.adlerplanetarium.org

Field Museum of Natural History
Chicago, Illinois
http://www.fieldmuseum.org

Museum of Science and Industry
Chicago, Illinois
http://www.msichicago.org

Pacific Science Center
Seattle, Washington
http://www.pacsci.org

Science Museum of Minnesota
St. Paul, Minnesota
http://www.smm.org

Smithsonian Institution
Washington, DC
http://www.si.edu

Canada
Canada Science and Technology Museum
Ottawa, Ontario
http://www.sciencetech.technomuses.ca

Provincial Museum of Alberta
Edmonton, Alberta
http://www.pma.edmonton.ab.ca

Index